1 MONTH OF
FREE
READING

at

www.ForgottenBooks.com

By purchasing this book you are eligible for one month membership to ForgottenBooks.com, giving you unlimited access to our entire collection of over 1,000,000 titles via our web site and mobile apps.

To claim your free month visit:
www.forgottenbooks.com/free195127

ISBN 978-0-484-59896-5
PIBN 10195127

ORGANIZED DISCUSSION

by

J. WINDSOR MUSSON, M.A., DIP. ED.,

Author of
Reading and Reasoning

—

*" The liberty of discussion is the great
safeguard of all other liberties "—*
(MACAULAY)

JOHN CROWTHER (EDUCATIONAL) LTD.
BOGNOR REGIS, SUSSEX

BY THE SAME AUTHOR

READING AND REASONING

*A course in intelligent reading
and comprehension of the spoken and
written word*

FOREWORD

IT is one of the basic principles of democracy that decisions are reached by discussion and consequent agreement, and are not the final judgment of one individual to be then made binding on the rest of the community.

This book was written to give some idea of the method whereby a satisfactory decision can be reached by what is known as the " Discussion Group " method. To conduct a discussion properly, so that it may bear fruit, requires an understanding of the technique involved, for there *is* a very definite technique, a certain amount of ingenuity and imagination. Given these, the leader of a group can ensure that all those taking part will have received a very valuable insight into the very nature of the democratic principle itself. They will have seen it at work, and, in addition, will not only have added to their own and the others' store of knowledge, but will also have had practice in the correct method of conducting an argument and exercising their reasoning powers.

Discussions should, therefore, form a part of every English syllabus ; they are valuable training for youth groups and are suitable for inclusion in W.E.A. and other adult education programmes, where they could follow lectures or lecture courses.

Throughout this book stress has been laid on the necessity for the organization of discussions. Some preparation is necessary for success, and a nation used to arriving at decisions by discussion and agreement will never willingly allow itself to be dragooned into registering approval of someone else's opinion by blind unthinking acceptance.

It is not too much to claim that if this book is under-standingly used a contribution will have been made, in no small measure, to the furtherance of this ideal.

I have to acknowledge with grateful thanks the help rendered by Miss J. Charatan, A.T.S., in the preparation of the MS. of this book.   J. W. M.

CONTENTS

5

CHAPTER I

How to Run a Discussion Group

1. What a Discussion Group is

It may sound rather an obvious remark to make, that before discussing or writing on any subject one should know exactly what it is one is talking or writing about. Yet this cardinal principle is very often neglected, and particularly so in the case of discussions. So often people stage what they imagine to be discussions, which are nothing but travesties of the real thing. It is the purpose of this book to show clearly what a discussion should be, in the hope that those who engage in this method of receiving and imparting instruction will get more from it than might otherwise have been the case.

The Discussion-Group method of instruction is a definite technique; it has its own rules and principles, simple ones, but ones that must be understood and practised. This is a point which cannot be too often stressed. Before this technique is explained, however, it is necessary, in the light of what has been said above, to obtain a clear picture of the nature of such a group.

A Discussion Group may be defined as a group of people, preferably containing from ten to twenty, brought together to discuss, by exchange of opinion, a set subject, under the direction of a leader. The various features of this definition will be considered in turn.

It was stated that the method of the discussion was " by exchange of opinion "—that is the purpose of a discussion; to bring opinions, to offer them for consideration, and to receive others in exchange. This rules out the individual who has no desire to learn; but who wants only to foist his own ideas on others. Humility should be one of the characteristics of those taking part. It follows that an individual adopting the correct attitude

7

has come to learn by testing the validity of his own ideas by considering those of others. He desires to be better informed, and to resolve such difficulties as he may have. Thus, the purpose of this method of instruction cannot be fulfilled if any individual sits back and says nothing. All must take part, and contribute according to their experience and ability, if the discussion is to be a success.

Now, the result of the efficient practice of this method is two-fold. Those participating increase their knowledge, and that is valuable; but what is more valuable still is that they learn to disagree, and that is one of the features of democracy, that one is allowed to dissent, and that such dissention is treated with respect. This technique is the democratic method of tackling problems, and because of this is one which should be practised whenever the opportunity occurs.

It often happens that at a discussion an individual is introduced for the first time to a new aspect of a subject, or he may suddenly realize how scanty was his knowledge, and how little he was able to say in comparison with what he would have liked to have said. Curiosity is thus often aroused, and people are driven to learn as a result of such a revelation. They are also made, by the very nature of the method itself, to accustom themselves to the exercise of their reasoning powers. Where passions are roused, reason holds little sway; in the calm atmosphere of the discussion, however, where the personal element is always discouraged, reason can find its rightful place. Thus, a discussion is primarily the orderly consideration of a set of facts presented by the leader, and the expression of opinions about them. This cannot be achieved, unless the reasoning faculties are fully exercised.

How often we are called upon to witness what a discussion most definitely is not. Sometimes it would appear to be a free-for-all-fight, where no order is observed, and the members set on one another in a desperate attempt, not to prove the validity of what they contend, but often

8

to persuade, or compel agreement with views they most tenaciously hold. At other times, it is still a fight, but in this case between two individuals who hold the floor by violent argument, the others being reduced to observing an enforced silence. Occasionally the leader takes it upon himself to deliver a lecture, at the end of which, perhaps some five minutes, may be devoted to expression of opinion. All these practices are unhelpful, and should never be allowed to mar the success of a discussion group.

At this point, it might be helpful briefly to consider the difference between the discussion and the debate. The main difference is that the latter is marked by great formality. The subject is supported by a Proposer and Seconder, and opposed by two speakers. The very atmosphere of formality often tends to discourage what is essential, namely, a steady flow of speakers. Instead, the discussion should be marked by informality and comfort. The choice of a suitable place in which to hold the group meeting is essential. Order must not, of course, be sacrificed to informality, but under good leadership, the two should be present. Controversy is essential to the debate, while this is not the case for all discussions. They may concern themselves with the attempt to discover more about a subject by the pooling of information.

It will be realized by now that a very great deal depends on the leader of a group, as to whether the discussion method is a success or not. He should be carefully chosen, and should especially be one who knows the technique as outlined here. Otherwise, however willing, he cannot properly fulfil his function.

2.   How to Conduct a Discussion

In our definition with which we started, the words " under the direction of a leader " occurred. A leader is literally a director, a conductor of the course of the discussion.

Now, there is a rule to be remembered by every leader. It is one he may not like to obey, or may find difficult to obey, but it is one which must always be observed, and cannot be too strongly stressed. The leader will on no account allow himself to be involved in the discussion in any way.

He is not there to express his opinions, but to be the medium by which opinions are circulated to the group. He is a referee, a chairman, a sifter of material presented to him, and nothing must cause him to forget this.

The leader will open the discussion in one of the ways to be stated later ; he then is offered a remark. All remarks are directed to him, for the obvious reason that thereby the discussion is maintained more on an impersonal level, for there is less danger, by this method, of personalities coming into conflict. Suppose A starts off with the remark : " I think many more flats ought to be built after the War," which is his first contribution to a discussion on housing. The leader thanks him, or acknowledges the contribution, and perhaps re-states it in such terms as : " We have had one opinion. Now, who feels otherwise ? " The discussion proceeds as follows :

B. " I don't like flats—we ought to have more detached houses. That's what people want."

L. " Now, ladies and gentlemen, we have had two diametrically-opposed views—flats *versus* houses."

C. " I think flats ought to be built in towns, and houses in the country."

L. " Thank you. C wants to modify the two views we've had. So that gives us a third possibility."

D. " Flats are better for towns because available space is less, but I think we can have them in the country too. I don't see why not."

L. " D is unable to see why you can't have flats in the country. Now who can settle his difficulty for him ; or do you think it is either impossible or impracticable to build them there ? "

From this illustration, .it will be seen that the leader never allows the discussion to get beyond his control. He is master of the situation, receiving, clarifying, or re-stating, and inviting comment as and when he thinks necessary. After several divergent views have been received, and opinions expressed by the group, the leader should summarize the position to date, so that members of the group may realize more clearly than might otherwise have been the case, what is the actual position.

It is obvious that such being the conception of the leader's function, it is only too easy for him to impose his own pattern on the discussion, and direct it arbitrarily along channels of his own choice. However great the temptation, this he must on no account do. He trims, and sifts, but the members determine the trend the remarks will take.

There are times, however, when the leader must influence, to a certain extent, the form of the discussion. Should a discussion flag for any reason, the leader must obviously revive it. There are several good ways of doing this; one is to consider the views already advanced. If one particular aspect of the subject has not been mentioned, he must introduce it by such a remark as, "I don't think anyone has considered this point of view——." It is, of course, unnecessary for him to hold this particular view himself, but, as we shall see, he must be knowledgeable about the subject, and this is where such knowledge can be put to excellent use. To make it clear that he is not trying to foist an opinion of his own, he can say, "There is a small (or large) group of people who believe most fervently that ——."

It may well happen that no one has any opinion to express on this new aspect; in that case " shock tactics " often prove successful. This means that the leader will ask individuals by name to give their views, or what is very valuable and effective, he will call on some person to give an account of a particular experience which may have a bearing on the discussion in question. The leader should therefore know, whenever possible, something about the background of the members of the group, so that he is in a position, at any time, to tap specialized knowledge. The point of view of the specialist can often be used to check a general impression—perhaps quite an erroneous one—which may have arisen.

This method of calling upon individuals should also be used to ensure that all are brought into the discussion. It is most desirable that there should be no " passengers," and with a little tact and patience even the most retiring can be made to contribute their share to the common pool of knowledge. The converse is also true. There may well be one who talks too much, or too often. The exuberant and aggressive will spoil the success of any group, and must be discouraged.

Another fault in speakers, which must be watched, is the tendency to irrelevance. This is fatal, for it breeds boredom and antagonism to the individual. Personalities then start to enter the picture. Such irrelevance must be checked, kindly but firmly. This is easy if the leader himself is really anxious to find out all that can be discovered about the subject under discussion. He will then naturally break in by saying, " But where does what you are saying get us ? I feel it doesn't quite bear on our subject."

Again, it may be that a speaker's statement is vague and needs clarification. This can be remedied if the leader makes such a remark as, " Now, you've all heard what B has said. Does that help you at all ? Do you all understand what he was getting at ? " Or," Who found that a little difficult to follow ? " There are answers of, " I did ! " Then the speaker is asked to make his point more clearly, or the leader can ask for confirmation that he has understood correctly by saying, " Now, do I understand you to mean —— ? "

It must be pointed out, however, that every opinion offered, however absurd, must be treated with respect if people are to be encouraged to talk. If a suggestion is received scornfully by the leader, the person who made it is likely to keep quiet for the rest of the discussion, and probably will not come again, making the obvious remark, " I didn't come here to be insulted,"—or, " My opinion's as good as his anyway." Tact is very necessary, especially when a group consists of persons of different social or educational levels.

Sometimes the members will turn on the leader and proceed to catechize him. This must not be allowed. He will not allow himself to be drawn into the argument, but will put the questions to the group for an answer. This is important, as many discussions are spoiled by back-chat between the leader and another member.

To be a success, a discussion must be arranged and prepared for beforehand. Spontaneous discussions do arise, and very good they often are ; but lack of suitable preparation on the part of the leader and group often means a waste of everyone's time. The subject should be known by all, some time beforehand, and the leader should have put in a little preliminary spade-work beforehand. He must know something about the subject, must understand some of the implications involved, and must realize when an important point has not been raised by anyone, or some vital aspect overlooked. This will be seen to be necessary when we come to consider later the method of introducing the subject. Let it suffice to say here that two things are necessary in a leader—a mastery of the technique of the discussion group, and a working knowledge (not necessarily extensive) of the subject with which he is concerned. He must know what he wants his members to talk about, and how he wants them to talk. Therefore, the position of leader must be filled with care.

3. The Subject—Its Choice and Introduction

The choice of a subject for a discussion is very important. There are some subjects which are not at all suitable for this purpose, and however well-intentioned the members may be they will make little headway.

A discussion is concerned with opinions, and opinions are formed about facts ; and this must be clearly understood before a discussion is embarked on. It is useless to announce a subject as : " Spain." You cannot discuss Spain *qua* Spain. You can discuss opinions, which people may have about aspects of Spanish life, but that is a very different matter. You can discuss why Spain is backward in its educational programme (if it is, the statement must be proved by production of supporting facts), or should Spain remain neutral, but even then such a subject demands a certain amount of specialized knowledge, which the group may not possess. The leader could supply it in his introductory talk, to be mentioned later, but even then, unless the members know something about the genera political and social background, the little knowledge they were given by the leader would indeed prove a dangerous thing. It should be considered axiomatic that the subject should be suited to the audience, and not the contrary. With the average intelligent adult audience, and with a · Youth group, a subject which touches their lives at as many points as possible should be chosen, and specialist subjects left for those more qualified to discuss them.

The subject chosen should not be vague, and a definite issue should be presented. The wording of the subject should be carefully considered. Thus, it is unwise to announce as a subject : " Prison Reform." It is better to be more particular, and introduce it in such terms as, " Are we too lenient in our treatment of criminals ? " This tends to keep out irrelevance, and ensures that everyone starts from the same place. If you are advertising a meeting, it is essential to say where you are going to meet. So with discussion subjects, as has been said above, you should know *precisely* what you want to talk about.

An alternative type of subject is to pose a question, such as, " What is a Gentleman? " and seek to arrive at a definition satisfactory to the majority. This is excellent as a training in reasoned thinking, especially on the part of the leader, who has all the time to see the wood as well as the trees.

A good subject can, however, be spoiled by a poor start, and the discussion may flag as a result. From the beginning interest must be aroused. If members have come voluntarily, the subject having been announced beforehand, it may be assumed that the interest is there ; but if a discussion is held regularly as part of a syllabus, such interest may have to be aroused. There are various ways of doing this, and the leader should vary his approach ; otherwise, if the same method is used over and over again, it will lose its effect.

The most frequent method is for the leader, or a member of the group, to introduce the subject by means of a short introductory talk. The function of this talk should be to make clear the points at issue, and to supply some facts which are necessary if the discussion is going to have a real basis. The release of so much " hot-air " is of little help to anyone. Let the speaker, then, very *briefly*, arouse interest, and give the necessary factual framework which the group will fill in from their own experience. Its length will be determined by the nature of the subject, and the intelligence of the audience. It should never exceed one-third of the total time available. It will often concern itself with statistics and figures, so that the subsequent discussion will bear relation to facts, and not to suppositions.

A lively discussion can often be provoked by the leader if he states forcibly a heretical opinion—not, of course, as his own but as one which he knows to be held in certain quarters. Or again, as we have seen, a direct question put to an individual (who can be warned beforehand to have an answer ready) may serve to break the ice.

Another method often used is to get four members or more to say a few words on some aspect of a topic, or to state shortly their individual opinions, and why they hold them. They, too, will have been approached beforehand, and will have come prepared. Their views will be offered by the leader to the group for comment, and as a result the four speakers may be called upon to defend or enlarge upon what they have said.

In a discussion on Housing, the leader asked the members—young people attending a Youth Club—each to bring a cutting from a paper or magazine dealing with a feature that was considered desirable. According to the type of improvement produced, so was the trend of the discussion determined. As a variation of this, in a discussion of the " What is a Gentleman ? " type, members could be asked to come prepared to give a definition. These could be listed on a blackboard (here let me say that an adequate blackboard is a great asset in the conduct of discussion) under headings, and would serve to keep the subsequent discussion on the right lines.

As well as a blackboard, diagrams and pictures can be used to introduce a subject, often with considerable effect. A diagram with a query written on the blackboard beside it may provoke a question, which the leader will have answered. Or he might invite attention to the blackboard, and ask if the group agree with whatever is written there. Soon the discussion is under way.

Supposing the discussion is to be about the treatment fo crime, the leader could exhibit a picture, say, of a prison cell in the last century, or of the gallows. He could then make the remark, " The other day I heard someone say that hanging was too good for some people, when they saw this picture. What do you feel ? " This appeal for their opinion must have the air of genuineness. If the leader really appears to want to know what A or B is thinking, then their opinions are likely to be far more quickly forthcoming than would otherwise be the case. Such a method tends to keep the discussion centralized, and gives it a link with reality. Someone has actually said something about a picture they are looking at. This takes it out of the realm of the merely abstract.

4. Ending a Discussion

All discussion, like stories and articles, should have a beginning, a middle, and an end. They are often denied the latter.

When the leader feels that the discussion has exhausted the subject, or that no more time is available, he will summarize the position reached, and make clear all the points at issue. He may be able to reconcile opinions, which at first might seem contradictory. The group can then be asked to state their preference by a show of hands for this or that view, and the discussion will end by a final re-statement of the result. Then, and not until then, the leader may, if he likes, state his opinion.

This does not pretend to be an exhaustive account of the technique of discussion, but the main points have been considered, and it is felt that if they are adhered to, a discussion cannot but be a success.

This, then, is the method of running a discussion group.

CHAPTER II

Five Discussion Themes Analysed

Method of Introduction by Leader Illustrated and Points of View Examined

Our purpose is this chapter is to indicate how each of five themes may be treated in actual discussion. From the material given the leader can see what points are likely to be brought up by members of the discussion group as well as those points which they may overlook. Using the methods outlined in Chapter I the leader can direct the attention of the group to any points of view they have omitted to raise.

It may be that a particular point attracts a considerable amount of interest. If this happens the discussion could centre around this point and not around the topic originally suggested. The leader should not feel himself bound completely by his pre-conceived line of approach. What is important is that some point of general interest shall be discussed according to the method already suggested.

The material given below is suitable for many discussions according to where the emphasis is placed. For example, Discussion No. 1 has as its main theme the relation between crime and punishment, and this theme might take *one* of the following forms :

(1) Is Prison Reform Necessary ?

(2) Is Society and not the Criminal at Fault ?

(3) Should Punishment be Merely Deterrent ?

(4) Our Present Methods of Punishing Crime are too Lenient.

(5) How should Juvenile Crime be Treated ?

And so with other themes. The raw material will be given, and it is for the leader to decide what to select and how best to introduce the subject. It should be noted, however, that for these five discussions a general theme only has been supplied ; the discussion centring around a particular aspect of that theme must have a specific title to be chosen by the leader. As has been said above, a group cannot be adequately prepared for a discussion if given only a vague theme.

DISCUSSION NO. 1

General Theme : CRIME AND PUNISHMENT

Introduction

This will, of course, depend on where the emphasis is placed. One method would be to choose a crime, such as the stealing of a sheep ; one member could describe how this would have been punished a hundred years ago ;

another could state how the criminal would probably be treated nowadays; while a third could outline the psychological or remedial treatment. The group would then be invited to make their comments.

As an alternative method a picture of a prison cell in the eighteenth or nineteenth century might be exhibited, showing how prisoners were ill-fed and crowded together. Point to this and say : " My little boy saw that picture the other day and asked me how could anyone be so cruel. What do you think I ought to have said to him ? "

The Material

Our Present Method of Treatment of Crime

It all depends upon what a man has done. Punishment is relative, and we have hit upon a rough and ready method of relating crime to punishment. To kill a man for stealing a sheep is cruel according to our present evaluation as to the relative enormity of offences.

Is our Method Correct ?

This will depend upon the conception of the purpose of punishment. It can be reformative or merely deterrent.

If the latter concept is held by the group they must consider the lengths to which such punishment should go. When does it become savage ? Is there a satisfactory " yardstick " ? Do the methods used by the Nazis have the desired deterrent effects ? Since " crimes " still occur it would appear that this is not entirely the case. What are the consequences of such savage punishment ?

If there is a schoolmaster present he could supply an answer.

Individuals are driven into opposition against those whom they consider oppressors. Boys become, in many cases, " Bolshie " and stubborn by harsh treatment. Such methods tend to sow the seeds of destruction which, when ripe, result in the accomplishment of the opposite of what is intended.

19

We have a definite scale of punishment based on a long line of judgments applied to similar cases. Judges are allowed a certain latitude, and there are always methods of appeal to higher authorities. The circumstances of the crime are taken into consideration and each case is dealt with on its merits. Is this deterrent ? Is that the intention of the judge when he passes sentence ? Who is deterred ? Are the members of the discussion group sufficiently frightened by the punishments inflicted to keep them from committing crime ? These are questions for the group to settle. Such phrases as : " Justice must be done " and " The public must be protected " give an indication as to our conception of the treatment of crime.

The Reformative Concept : (1) *Juvenile Crime*

This we do see at work in our treatment of young offenders. Consider the implications of the word " Reformatory," for instance, and also the patient efforts of the magistrates of juvenile courts. Ask for the opinion of those who may have had experience of work of this kind. Consider the rôle of the Probation Officer. Is there a great gap between theory and practice ? Refer to the Hereford case.

To settle points like these facts must be produced. The leader can obtain them either from books of reference, such as " Whitaker's Almanack," or from local sources.

Has juvenile crime diminished as a result of this more humane treatment ? Are there other reasons which might account for a drop (if there is one) in figures over a period of years ? If there is an increase, who or what is to blame ? What is being done about it, locally and nationally ?

(2) *Adult Crime*

Experiments have already been made in the direction of reformative treatment. Refer to the Russian experiment of the penal settlement at Bolshevo and to the Wakefield Prison Camp where there are no walls, and men are on their honour not to escape.

The Purpose of Reformative Treatment

The concept of crime held by the reformers is that it is a disease and should be treated as such. Refer to Butler's "Erewhon" for a similar idea. The desire is to cure the criminal and to restore a useful citizen to the State. Deterrent punishment will not cure; it will only restrain by fear. As there is a stigma attached to those who have been to prison the *status quo* is seldom attained.

Is a man punished by the State for deliberately allowing himself to catch a chill? Should he be? Refer to recent advertisements dealing with the absence from work of those who are sick. The idea of culpable neglect is being suggested by the advertisers.

Is it more reprehensible to commit a crime of passion? Why is the one considered a greater evil? Because of its result? Is a man punished because of motive or result of crime? Which should be the guiding factor?

The reformer believes that by suitable treatment the causes which made a man commit a crime can be removed and thus the temptation can be removed as well.

The Criminal and Society

Consider the view that crime is due to man's maladjustment between himself and the society in which he lives. Political crimes and stealing because of hunger are examples. Change the social environment and you will have changed the man is the contention of this group of thinkers.

Some Objections

The following points will probably be raised :

(1) This treatment will result in making it easier for people to commit crime because they know they will receive more lenient treatment.

(2) The very fact that more crime may result shows the need for extensive treatment of the criminal. Deterrent measures keep potential criminals from the knowledge of the community and from committing crime. Is it better that they should be discovered and cured or merely kept in check, no one knowing when they may break out?

(3) This will take time and, meanwhile, how are the public to be protected from the potential criminals as and when they break out into crime?

(4) There is no need to wait until crime has been committed until the cure is begun. Start by reforming the social surroundings of the individual; remove want and provide suitable occupation for leisure hours. Refer to war-time crimes committed because of a lack of things to do because of early closing of places of amusements and restaurants. "The Devil finds mischief for idle hands to do." Wrong employment is a source of crime. It breeds dissatisfaction and resentment against the social order.

DISCUSSION NO. 2

General Theme : WOMAN AND THE HOME

Method of Introduction

Choose several young people (preferably married), say, two men and two women, and get them to say what they feel about what women should do after the war—whether they should work or stay and look after the house. At the end of their talks summarize the divergent points of view.

Alternatively, list on the blackboard several well-known statements about women, such as :

(1) A woman's place is the home.

(2) Kinder, Kirche, Kuche· (children, church, kitchen—the three focal points of a woman's interest).

(3) A woman has a right to a career.

(4) The equality of the sexes.

The group should then investigate each of these so that the implications involved are recognized. For example, does No. 3 imply that to keep house and to be a mother is not a career ?

At the end of such a discussion show the danger of accepting and repeating such statements unless their implications are thoroughly understood, and all possible reasons for rejecting them have been considered. This is one of the valuable results of discussion groups ; it shows that to make a statement of opinion without having dissected it beforehand is dangerous and to be discouraged in oneself and others.

The Material

Origin of the Remarks quoted above

Who makes these statements ? Women themselves ? Men or both ? How is it known that they are made ? Conversation ? Newspapers ? Books ? Has any analysis of opinion been made by such methods as Mass Observation or the Gallup Poll ?

What is the Primary Function of a Woman ?

(1) Are all agreed that primarily she is the child-bearer and housekeeper ? Is the latter only applicable to previous periods when society was differently organized or is it as fundamental as the first ?

(2) There is a definite feeling, instinctive in many, that they don't like to see a woman work—that it is all wrong somehow. Is this because, for the first time, this position is being seriously challenged, and old ideas die hard ?

(3) If woman is primarily the child-bearer, should she also be the one to bring up the child ? How are we to ensure that she is properly qualified ? If she is to do this, for how long ? This will mean that she will be

23

mainly occupied in household duties because she will be tied to the home, at least during the early years. How much time and for how long should she remain at home? If she is not to rear the children, then who will? State nurseries with all that these imply or private nurses? This involves a consideration of the value of parental upbringing which is a subject in itself. Salient points are:

(a) Is the parent qualified to rear children? Has she a knowledge of the nature of a child mind, and does she know that the lines along which she wishes it to develop are the best? Should the child develop with an absolute minimum of parental interference?

(b) Are the home conditions conducive to proper upbringing? Is the food provided adequate and of the right kind? Is the arrangement of the house suitable? Is the mother likely to take the child out late at night because she is too selfish to stay at home and see that it goes to bed at the proper time? Can we ensure that women will have children because they want to love and care for them, or are they mere incidentals to physical satisfaction?

Women who Do not want Children or who Cannot have Them

If there is no fundamental objection to their staying at home then the following points must be considered:

(1) Who is going to look after the house?

(2) Can a woman or a man after a hard day's work be expected to spend some time in preparation of meals and housework?

(3) Solution—either have some sort of domestic help or eat in a restaurant. Flats with restaurants attached offer a remedy. What is the position of those who live in the country?

The Unmarried Woman

(1) If there is a stigma attached to a woman's earning her own living, what is this class of woman going to do ? Will she be forced to seek marriage to engage in the only type of activity permitted her ?

(2) If it is agreed that at least this type should seek work, of what kind shall it be ? Are all jobs to be open ? Jobs that are not. The Church of England does not permit women rectors ; female medical students are limited to a small quota. There are few women barristers and no women judges. What will be the effect of the enrolment of women in the Services ? Will certain jobs still be regarded as the male prerogative ? Can a woman do all types of work as successfully as men, manual labour excepted ? Jobs done by women during the war—what has this shown ? N.F.S., Civil Defence, Mixed Gun Sites. Have women withstood the strain as well as men ?

(3) At the last census taken there were in the country ten and a quarter million women and girls, six million of whom were earning their own living. It would seem that it is established that some women, at any rate, should work. These questions arise :

(a) Are they to be paid as much as men ? They could be, if a system of marriage allowances was introduced, and the salaries of single men and women were equated.

(b) Are they to be allowed to retain their posts when they marry ? Refer to attitude of some Education Committees who will not employ in peace-time married schoolmistresses.

(c) Education of girls tends to be based on the assumption that they are potential wives—classes in Domestic Science, Needlework, Mothercraft are given. If a girl has no intention of being married there should be alternatives, and a curriculum which prepares for an occupation. Motherhood should be regarded, from the educational point of view, as one of the many possible occupations.

Effects of a Woman's being Occupied other than in the Home

(1) Increase in " mannishness "—dress, manners ?

(2) Is there a danger of men becoming not merely equals but inferior ? This is based on the assumption that men are superior. Is this mere fiction ?

(3) The importance of the home may become less, and the French concept may be adopted of a home as a place to sleep in and nothing else.

(4) Will the adoption of some of these views mean the decay of family life ? The stages are :

  (1) Large Victorian families.

  (2) Smaller twentieth century families.

  (3) Far fewer post-war ones ?

DISCUSSION NO. 3

General Theme : GERMANY'S NEW ORDER

Method of Introduction

A display of contrasting pairs of pictures would be an effective method of introducing the subject. These can be obtained from *Picture Post* or any similar magazine or from an illustrated newspaper.

A series of well chosen pairs—such as an English schoolboy, say, in cricket flannels and a photo of a member of the Hitler Youth ; a crowd in Hyde Park and a picture of a Nazi Party rally ; scenes depicting the invasion of Austria, treatment of Jews, etc., are suitable. Let the group study these, and listen to their comments. If these can be made the basis of a discussion, so much the better ; if not, ask for opinions as to the nature and reason for the contrast.

The Material

What are the Features of the New Order ?

(1) Hitler wanted to make Germany self-sufficient ; she was to be an industrialized nation ; other European

States were to be vassals supplying her with food in exchange for manufactured goods.

(2) Germany is the master race and superior to all others.

(3) The individual exists not for himself but for the State, to which he must place himself in complete subjection.

These Features Considered

(1) (*a*) History has been marked, since the Industrial Revolution particularly, by a struggle between industrialized nations for markets and for trade domination. This has caused friction and wars ; cut-throat competition and anything but the peace we are seeking. Although not the only cause of war, it is one of the main ones, having as its root greed and desire for individual gain at the expense of another.

(*b*) Germany has provided a solution to this problem by endeavouring to ensure that the only markets were her own. The first stage was to build up an industrial machine ; then to conquer by force, if necessary, if not by penetration and collapse from within. To ensure that there would be no rivals a rôle would be assigned to all other States, mainly that of producing food and buying or receiving in exchange for food given to Germany the latter's manufactured products. Refer to exports of aspirins and mouth-organs to the Balkans before this war.

. (*c*) This meant certainly the solution to the problem of international rivalry and, provided Germany retained her dominant position, there would certainly be no more war—for the various States would not have the equipment with which to fight.

(*d*) The price which would be paid would be considerable. It would mean a method and standard of living for all non-Germans dictated by the Germans ; the loss to each State of her self-government and national way of life ; and the acceptance of a position somewhat

27

akin to that of the medieval serf. One's work and the way it was to be conducted would be imposed by the " master race," and it is doubtful if anything but a bare minimum standard of living would be allowed.

(e) But there would be co-operation—enforced, admittedly—and organization on an international scale. These are essential qualities for a post-war order. Can they be secured other than by force ?

(f) There must be some limitation of individual ability to do as one likes, because there must be loyalty to an ideal higher than that of providing for oneself or one's family which, in the majority of cases to-day, is the incentive which drives many to earn a living. In the German slave-order the maintenance of the German people in comfort is the " ideal." Fear of the consequences of disobedience enforces compliance. Substitute as the ideal maintenance of the comfort of all *other* peoples ; let this be the incentive ; let fear of harming others by failure to produce the very best of which one is capable and a delight in work itself inspire all one does. In this way the problem is solved and no harmful results are the consequence.

(g) As long as our political and economic organization is based on units, each out-bidding the other—or linked in an uneasy partnership dictated by fear, war will continue. The German New Order has provided a hint as to a solution, but has gone about it from wrong motives and in the wrong way. The solution lies in all working for the good of the whole, and being thus willing to disregard individual preferences, " seeking their own in another's good."

(2) The Germans are admittedly motivated by self-interest. The peace-time economy must guarantee to Germany a maximum of economic security and to the German people a maximum consumption of goods. This is also the aim of other States, only they do not state it so bluntly. The Germans and the Japanese do also believe

in racial superiority. They have an ideal that it is their mission to rule the world as the master races. This is the cause of the fanaticism displayed by German and Japanese. It lifts them out of self and endows them with superhuman energy. This ideal is constantly before them ; from the cradle to the grave they are not allowed to forget it. Therefore they endeavour to behave so as to be " worthy " of the master-race of which they are members, not to be bettered by an inferior race.

Refer to Leader Schools, where political leaders are trained who watch the civilian population for any act which would make a German " unworthy " of his race (grumbling, criticism, etc.).

Have we, as a nation, any positive ideal ? Have we a driving force capable of sustaining us and making us able to endure hardship ? We talk about democracy and praise it, but are we enthusiastic about it ? Do we tell foreigners about this excellent system which we have ? Have we a way of life ? Refer to the Nazi conception of " weltanschaung " or the Nazi world outlook. Can we hope to succeed unless we have a spiritual driving force ? Are the churches realizing this ? In Germany the church was disregarded and a Nazi conception of religion substituted for Christianity. We have an adequate ideal in the Christian teaching, but how should it be related to the everyday problems of life ? Can the Nazi method teach us anything ? The new Education Bill attempts a solution by insisting on religious instruction. Is this enough ? Is not example the best form of advertisement ?

(3) This third feature results in the co-ordination of all activities under State direction. It ensures uniformity and the impossibility of opposition.

However much we dislike regimentation we must ask and answer the question : " Why and for what do we exist ? " Should we reply : " To glorify by our work the State," as does the German, or " To glorify the God who made us " ? Is there no reason why a man should exist ? Is to please oneself a legitimate end in life ?

Refer to the Puritan attempt to establish a theocracy by something like Nazi methods, and its faliure.

The German people can be driven. We have to be led. Are there any leaders to-day who have the vision and energy to lead us ?

If we are to give service to an ideal, then that ideal must dominate our every activity. There is nothing wrong with subordination to the State providing that the purpose behind it is approved by the individual, and that efficiency is gained and that such subordination is essential (e.g., in war-time).

DISCUSSION NO. 4

General Theme : Social Security

Method of Introduction

Be concrete ; touch the lives of your audience here as elsewhere. Don't be too abstract in your introduction. Let general principles be evolved from concrete illustrations.

Start off with some forthright questions such as :

(1) I know an old woman of seventy. She thinks she isn't getting enough Old Age Pension. How much ought she to get ? What are the necessary qualifications ?

(2) Can a man who was earning £600 a year and has to retire through illness get any financial help from the State ?

(3) People who earn more than £420 a year are left out of existing National Health and Unemployment schemes. Is this right ?

(4) If we pay our N.H.I. contributions and never need sick or unemployment benefit, ought we to have some of our contributions refunded ?

(5) If you insure people against want and sickness, does this tend to make them lazy ?

30

The Material

Underlying Principles

There are two implied in the answers to these questions :

(1) (*a*) If a person knows his future is secure because he is insured against want and sickness, will he, being human, tend not to put forth his best, and become lazy ? Is the necessity to provide for oneself the most powerful incentive to work ?

(*b*) Why should the State look after one in sickness and need if one is working for oneself, and solely for one's own benefit ?

(2) Any scheme of social security must ensure that maximum effort is always maintained when a man is in work. There must be some method whereby, if a man is dismissed by an employer for bad work, this fact will be notified to the authorities, and if a similar dismissal is subsequently recorded, then a certain proportion, or all of the pension to be received on retirement should be withheld.

(3) It must be decided why the State should concern itself with Social Security. If it is held that the State is the employer of all, then very generous provisions should be made. If not, then whatever benefits are provided are surely generous but not essential gestures on the State's part. It is essential to decide whether an individual has a right to social security ; if he has not, then he has no right to demand it at all.

(4) Opposed to the idea that it is a man's duty to earn a living for himself and his family, and to save to provide against sickness, old age, etc., is the view that much of what happens to him is entirely beyond his control. In the industrialized world of to-day, national policies, framed by statesmen, may involve unemployment for many. It is, therefore, considered neither just nor good sense to make a man suffer for what he cannot control. The State, therefore, undertakes to take over the work

previously performed by voluntary bodies, not as though recognizing a right on the part of the population to help, but as a matter of practical politics.

Features of Social Security Schemes

(The details of the Beveridge Plan will have either been circulated or explained before the discussion takes place).

(1) Should benefit be dependent on the means of the individual ? Insurance as provided by the Insurance Companies takes no notice of an individual's resources. Present unemployment benefit subject to a " Means Test " but not Sick Benefit. Is it right that under the proposed Beveridge Scheme a man should receive a weekly sum, irrespective of whether he needs it or not ? Part of this sum is made up of his contributions, but part is public money.

(2) The Scheme is designed to include everybody. Is this necessary ? Should those who are not likely to benefit (because they do not need financial assistance owing to their high income level) pay in order that those who do need may receive help ? This contribution is not taxation to pay for many amenities, but a levy to meet a specific type of expenditure. Should insurance against sickness and unemployment be compulsory at all ? Should the individual be allowed to take the risk, as in the case of, say, insurance against theft or fire ?

(3) Pensions (other than industrial) advocated by the Beveridge Scheme are dependant on retirement; the pensions introduced by the New Zealand Government are not. Which should be the case ?

Social Security. When ?

There will be many plans awaiting to be put into operation after the War, and the question will arise as to which should receive priority ? How far up in the list should a Social Security plan come ?

The Question of Cost. The estimated cost of social insurance under the Beveridge Scheme in 1945 is put at £367 millions, and in 1965 at £553 millions; this provides Unemployment Benefit, Retirement Pensions, Marriage and Funeral Grants, etc. The cost of National Assistance, which includes Health and Rehabilitation Services, Children's Allowances, etc., is estimated to be in 1945, £697 millions, and in 1965, £858 millions. Can the country afford the burden of such heavy expenditure? Would the additional taxation involved cripple industry? This is but one of the costs to be borne after the war. Consider the cost of the Education and Housing Schemes? Our payment for the war is partly made possible by contracting debts; if there is to be fresh heavy expenditure, will there be a limit to the amount of money that can be raised?

Note.—To tackle this, it is better that an expert give a few remarks on how a nation pays for any great undertaking. If the discussion is carried on by people who do not understand the principles of finance, it will be useless. There should be someone in the district who could give the required help. Because of lack of knowledge, a great deal of nonsense can be talked about finance, which is a very tricky subject.

Instead of the method suggested above, the leader could take the proposals as outlined in the Official Report published by the Stationery Office, and state the proposals one by one. The members of the group could discuss these, and then pass, amend, or reject them. This could only be done provided the principle that the State should undertake the provision of social insurance, was agreed, or assumed.

Such a discussion could follow one which dealt with the general principles of Social Security as a whole, which have been outlined above, and not with any specific scheme.

Method of Introduction

Ask each member of the group to state a form of control exercised by the Government, which in some measure restricts our life. Summarize these on the blackboard, under such headings as " Finance," " Transport," " Food," etc. Then ask if there is any aspect of life which is not subject to control. Again ask members to state a control they consider unnecessary, or, alternatively, eminently desirable. Finally, ask them to give reasons for their answers.

The Material.

The Purpose of Control

Co-ordination of all activities towards a desirable end makes it imperative that any activity that endangers the success of the effort must be restricted or forbidden. This is the old paradox of saving one's life by losing it. If, for example, all the metal which can be spared is needed for armament production, then obviously lead cannot be allowed to be made into toy soldiers, as the need is greater for the former than for the latter. Therefore, the uses to which manufacturers will put lead must be controlled.

This is largely accepted because the reason is seen.

Post-War Control

(1) Is the need for control after the war as urgent as before ? Is there a similar need to co-ordinate all activities towards a common end, as is seen during a War ? Could the ideal of an adequate distribution of food and services be made a common goal ? As soon as the war is over, will there be a desire to be free from as many restrictions as possible ? This means either un-co-ordinated activity— every man engaging in business as and how he can, or co-ordination of activity of large groups—combines—each

of which has a definite aim and enforces control over its members.

(2) What controls can obviously be relaxed ? Detention under 18B ? Travelling restrictions, lighting restrictions ? Refer to restrictions of last war never removed, i.e., items in Defence of Realm Act.

(3) The Government plans for reconstruction, and their decision as to what schemes will be given priority will determine the general plan that control will take, i.e., restrictions in location of industry and land development. Refer to Uthwatt, Barlow and Scott Reports.

(4) The position of private enterprise. What will the situation be ? Will it be allowed free rein ? Should the wasteful system of several shops selling the same things, i.e., newspapers, confectionery, tobacco, in the same area, be allowed ?

(5) The Beveridge Plan provides that if a man cannot obtain employment for himself, he must attend a training centre, and be directed to a somewhat limited choice of trade to adopt. This is control. Is it justified ? What is the criterion ? Should the large combines be subject to control—more so than they are now ?

(6) If economy is to be State-controlled, what will be the position of the Trade Unions ? Will they become subservient to higher authority ? In that case, would they have a function to perform ? Could they exist in an advisory capacity ?

(7) Does control on a wide scale mean employment and security for all ? Unemployment exists partly because of circumstances caused by competition and the consequent wastage that ensues.

Control and Incentive

(1) Will control mean that where it is applied all incentive to produce will disappear ? If the State controls and orders what shall be produced, what reason will there

be for the ceaseless experiments and research which characterize such concerns as Imperial Chemical Industries? There, the researcher is spurred on partly because he knows that he will be rewarded for success; the owner of a concern because he may be able to attract more business.

(2) If the people could feel that industry belonged to them, and that it was in their own interests to produce better and cheaper goods, there would be greater incentive than at present where the employee knows that the concern is not his own, and he has little personal interest in it. If the State rewarded such service, as in Russia, by according the outstanding worker a definite place in society—such as is accorded to-day to holders of Academic or Military distinctions—it could be ensured that public control would not kill enterprise.

Control—Disadvantages and Advantages of

Individual liberty restricted, often arbitrarily—bureaucratic muddle—refer to timber control of this war. Requisitioning of property at a moment's notice. Inadequate compensation? Danger of steam roller methods, which lead to the ignoring of the individual, who tends to become a mere cog in a machine.

Consider control in one branch of national life—housing. Designs will be to a certain extent standardized, prices and locations controlled; opportunity to exercise one's own choice as to place and style and material will be limited. Advantage: The speculative builder will be checked, and a good solid type of house will be provided. Would a government-controlled job be as speedily carried out as would a privately-sponsored one? Houses produced under a mass-produced scheme will be cheaper. We shall probably have a government-controlled scheme as to provision of houses, but also individuals may, if they like, and in certain areas, build their own houses, subject, perhaps, to certain price restrictions.

In all probability, we shall compromise, and allow a certain amount of control to go hand in hand with a certain amount of private initiative.

Refer to the newly-formed Society of Individualists, whose advertisements appear in *The Times*. Movements to fight control are already in being.

Some questions for consideration :

    (1) Does " Remove Control " mean : " Let me make profits as quickly as I can, and in any way I like ? "

    (2) Does lack of control mean chaos ?

    (3) Could such buildings as are seen in Peacehaven and Rottingdean have been produced had there been Government control of housing estates ?

    (4) Are control and " red - tape " necessarily synonymous ?

CHAPTER III

FORTY-FIVE CLASSIFIED DISCUSSION TOPICS. SHORT NOTES ON HOW THEY COULD BE TREATED

In this chapter forty-five discussion topics are suggested, and brief notes are added as indications to the leader as to possible lines on which they could be treated. There is much material to hand if the leader will only make use of it. Prolific sources are the correspondence columns of newspapers and magazines. *Picture Post*, the *Spectator*, the *New Statesman and Nation*, are very helpful in this respect. If the Parliamentary Reports in *The Times* are studied, material for many subjects can be found. The illustrated papers such as the *Daily Sketch* and the *Daily Mirror* contain many columns of opinion which can be put to good use.

The subjects given below have been divided into three sections : (*a*) Social and Economic, (*b*) Educational, and (*c*) Political. It must be emphasized that these notes mention only some of the points for consideration, and should not be considered by any means as exhaustive.

SECTION I—Social and Economic

1. What is a Gentleman?

Leader could read Newman's definition in his *Idea of a University*. The group could then discuss the " ingredients " necessary ; these could be listed on a blackboard. Certain suggestions would raise protests. Majority vote could be taken as to what should be included in the list. A current definition or•such phrases as " Nature's gentleman," could be analysed. This could lead to another discussion as to how the desired qualities could be inculcated in schools. This could lead on to the consideration of the difference between a Christian and a gentleman. Is it enough to be a gentleman ? Can one be a Christian and not be a gentleman ? This would be a version of the Ethics *versus* Christianity controversy.

2. Blood Sports should be Abolished

Get one member to state the case for abolition and one for retention ; this is a question of relative values. Is the profit to farmer, tailor, horsebreeder, refreshment concerns, etc., of more value than the well-being of the animal ? There is the question of the effect on the individual. Is it coarsening ? If foxes are pests should they not be painlessly destroyed ? Can deer hunting be excused ? Is there sadism in all of us♦and is its partial satisfaction likely to prove insufficient ? Is the next stage one similar to Jew baiting ? Are the motives the same ?

3. Hospitals should be State - Controlled and State - Maintained

Outline present system. Some State-supported, and some private and self-supporting. At present treatment, if given free, is of necessity not so good as that provided for paying patients ; similar position regarding accommodation. Thus those who can afford to pay receive better treatment. If the State maintained and controlled all hospitals, would the independence and pride in self-government of these institutions be lost ? Would their individuality and liberty to experiment along chosen lines be retained ? The individual can now choose his hospital and can ensure the best treatment, if he can pay for it. Could a State-controlled hospital be able to afford such a good standard of accommodation and care ? Owing to lack of funds, are many hospitals which are full obliged to allow treatment to suffer because of inadequacies of staff ? Are patients treated in rather a summary fashion and given scant attention ? Recent reports in the press *re* hospital food. What is the advantage of State maintenance ? Would State control reduce to a dead level ? Would this matter if this level were high enough ? Where will the money come from ? Insurance contributions to be increased ? Rates ? National tax ?

4. *Broadcasting should be made Competitive and not Monopolistic*

The leader could ask for comments as to the difference between the programmes formerly radiated by Radio Luxembourg and the B.B.C. programmes. Preference could be asked for. Competition means striving to win popular support by excellence of a product. The B.B.C. has monopoly, and however poor, can always count on support because there is no satisfactory alternative English programme. The B.B.C. is sensitive to public opinion, and does try to please the majority through Listener Research Department. Competitive private broadcasting depends on advertising. One is constantly being reminded of the fact. If advertisers paid high prices, would there be more money available to the B.B.C. for production of better programmes ? Does the B.B.C. control amount to a dictatorship ? What remedy have we if we don't like what is provided by the B.B.C. ? None, unless we can understand and receive foreign programmes. With competitive broadcasting, if sales drop because programmes are poor and people do not listen, thus resulting in falling sales, the company concerned has to find better material. If there are more programmes, choice is greater, and each section of the community can find its tastes catered for more widely. The B.B.C. at present subsidized by Government from pockets of taxpayers. Alternative, a private corporation owned by individuals.

5. Titles should be Abolished

Titles have no place in a democratic country ? Because they belong to a past age and to periods of privilege ? Do they serve any useful purpose ? Are they indications of services rendered to the State ? Position of hereditary titles. Snob reaction to a title. Soviet system where title is given as a reward for exceptional services rendered to the State. Is the gift of a large sum of money from a man who can afford it a service to the State ? Ought the titles conferred by Universities as a result of degrees earned be preferred to social ones ? Reaction against titles. Bishops who refuse to be called " My Lord," and peers who never use their titles.

6. Does the Press need Reforming ?

An excellent way to start this discussion is to display copies of about five different newspapers, to include such papers as *The Times*, *Daily Telegraph*, *Daily Express*, *Daily Sketch*, and *News-Chronicle*. Let the group study the different ways in which similar news items are presented. Then ask which methods are preferred and why.

What is meant by the Press ? Newspapers ? If so, distinguish between the popular Press and the more responsible papers. Consider the function of a newspaper. At present, the popular papers give the public what it wants. It meets them at their level. Should it endeavour gradually to reform their taste ? How would one refute the charge of dullness which would be levelled at the reforming paper ? The public likes excitement. What is the real nature of the news as presented ? Is it news in the usually accepted sense ? Will the public accept and like something better if it is offered ? *The Times* is threepence, which is more than many can afford, otherwise it might have a larger circulation. Should sensation and irrelevance be replaced by sober and true reports, not written up to catch the popular taste ?

When are papers read ? On the way to work, at meals, and after a hard day's work, by the majority. Are they then in a condition to read and follow anything presented in the way *The Times* reports the news ? *The Times* is not only a paper for the well-educated, but also for those who have the leisure time as well. Could its technique be adapted to meet the needs of the majority, i.e., for news soberly presented but easily and quickly assimilated ? Refer to Sunday papers. Are the same differences seen ? Is the need for quick assimilation the same ?

7. *Private Trading is Wasteful and Uneconomic*

The above is true only if there are not enough goods to balance demand. Thus labour is being used unproductively ; it might be put to better use. This is the case in war-time. All unproductive labour is put to productive use. Is the need as urgent after the war ?

Multiplication of small shops selling similar goods is uneconomic when distribution services are viewed as a whole. As long as distribution is privately arranged this will continue. If the State undertook such services the private trader would be replaced by large distributive concerns, such as the Co-operative Society. The private trader does serve a locality, and often saves the individual long journeys. One often has a link with the owner of the shop, and there is a personal element in the service rendered. Does a large store tend to be inhuman ? But one can get to know an employee there, as well as in a small shop. The multiplication of small shops causes the wholesaler many journeys to supply small quantities here and there. Do transport costs incurred by visits to so many scattered shops mean an increase in the price of the article ? Other price-increases caused by the private trader system.

Private trader often in competition with his neighbour. Because of his small capital, he cannot afford a wide range of goods.

8.   Has the Church Failed ?

This is a big, though a vital subject. It was recently tackled by a special series of services arranged by the Director of Religious Broadcasting. It is suggested that a clergyman be asked to open the discussion with a few words, and afterwards to wind up.

.What do we mean by the Church ? All Christian bodies, or only the Established Church ? What should the Church have done that some consider it has not done ? Stop wars and overcome poverty ? What is the function of the Church ? To change men's lives ? To provide access to God ? To be only the guardian and administrator of the Sacraments ? Should it change men by force ? Man himself is ultimately responsible for all social evils. The Church points the way, elaborating as it does the teachings of Jesus. It offers to help and strengthen, but man must make the decision to reform. The Church cannot make this for him. Has it failed because it is considered that it does not even point the way, teach the Gospel, or adequately strengthen and console ? Is it a failure everywhere, or in certain instances only ? How can these failures, if there are any, be remedied ? Divisions in the Christian Church. Do they impair its efficiency and success, or are all creeds united as to the remedies for social evils, and on major issues ?

9. . Should the Church of England be Disestablished ?

An introduction should be given setting forth the features of the government of an established church. King the theoretical head of the Church, Parliament the effectual head. Power of Parliament limited to discussion and rejection or acceptance of measures affecting the Church. Parliament cannot amend. The measures are framed by the Houses of Convocation of the two Provinces and presented to Parliament.

Disadvantages of the system. No real self-government by churchmen. Discussion and possible rejection of Church measures by M.P.s who are in many cases out of sympathy altogether with the Church of England. Some may be atheists or agnostics. Are they qualified to discuss and vote against measures affecting a body with which they are not concerned ?

Should Bishops, so vital to the welfare of the Church, be chosen by a politician who can easily override the suggestions of the Archbishop of Canterbury? Political choices. Farce of capitular elections of the King's nominee. Similar procedure in the case of Deans.

Does the phrase " A National Church," which is so often put forward as an argument in favour of establish-- ment, really mean anything ?

Advantages : An established church is financially better off. If disestablished, what would happen to tithes, glebe, etc. ? These are paid by virtue of a law which would be no longer binding. A non-national church could not expect to receive national financial support. State backing gives a church power to enforce its decisions.

10. *Post-War Britain : What Reconstruction Plans should have Priority ?*

What are the immediate post-war problems ? Feeding and housing the homeless in Europe ? Finding work for the demobilized ? Rebuilding in England what has been destroyed ? These are essentials. Are there any other essential needs ? To what extent should we help Europe at the expense of our own people ? Should all our food, surplus to our present ration, go to Europe ? Will labour.

for European reconstruction be largely provided by the inhabitants of each country ?

The work for the demobilized will depend on what reconstruction plans are being carried out. Every man cannot have his job back, as many concerns are no longer functioning. The plans to be considered first will depend on the type of persons first demobilized, or will the plan be decided first, and the right type then be released ? Will the type of scheme decided on as deserving priority depend on the amount of money available ? Will the people press urgently their claims sufficiently ? Refer to the failure of " Homes for Heroes " after the last war.

Probably housing and European reconstruction in which we shall play a part will come first ; increased food production,￭ and provision of agricultural machinery ; then manufacture of articles for export, as and when markets are found.

Education and social security. Where is the development of civil aviation and many other commercial schemes to be fitted in ? Will their sponsors agree to delay if they are not allowed to put their schemes into operation when they want to ?

The leader could first suggest an order of priority, and list it on the blackboard. Then the different suggestions could be compared and the group asked why certain places were allotted to certain schemes on the list.

11. *Post-War House Design. What Kind of Houses do we Want ?*

Migration to country, or re-planning the town ? Position of the new industries will determine place to a certain extent. Do we still want to live as individualists in a detached house of.our own, or in flats with communal restaurants, crêches, and other facilities attached ? Are we ready to change our concept of life to that of the community or group as the unit and not so much the family ? Are we still going to be content with the long

44

rows of mean houses ? Refer to successful housing estates, such as the Gas, Light and Coke Company's flats at Kensal Rise—with their nurseries and parks for children to play in. The flats should be separated by areas of grass and trees.

If a detached house is demanded, will pre-fabrication be employed to cope with the demand ? Will design of individual houses be uniform ? Should there be a unifying feature, or should unrestricted individual preference be allowed ? Will new housing designs be adopted—flat roofs, round shapes ? (The leader would do well to invite members to bring a picture of the type of house they would like ; let these be passed round, or exhibited to note common features.) What number of rooms are required ? Are there any new interior features that are demanded ? Heating ? Kitchen design ? Folding doors to divide one large living room into dining- and sitting-room ?

12. Do we Need a Ministry of Fine Arts ?

This Ministry exists abroad. The war has given rise to C.E.M.A. Provision of art exhibitions, concerts, good plays, etc., at present only possible in large cities, and where there is some assurance, if not of profit, at least of no big loss. Should these things be available for all ? C.E.M.A. provides travelling exhibitions. If all cultural activities were co-ordinated under a Ministry of Fine Arts, an adequate provision of cultural activities could be provided for all. At present—or before the war—this provision was haphazard. Then there was no endeavour on a wide scale to find new audiences, or to meet the known need in new and diverse ways. There were little local centres of activity, where the Director of Education and Curator of the local museum would encourage and organize art exhibitions, displays, concerts, etc. .Are such things vital necessities ? If so, should they be left to the initiative of the individual, and should they depend on

the provision of money, largely by subscription ? Refer
to present method of raising subscriptions before a concert
can be given ; or to the fact that to pay for a series of
concerts one *popular* item has often to be included in
the programme. Many theatres make up for losses on
classics by presenting variety during the Summer.

The war has shown that the people want these activities.
The decision must be made as to whether their provision
should be (*a*) permanent, and (*b*) provided and supervised
by the Government ; or left to private initiative.

13. *The only Social Distinction should be Distinction. of
Intellect*

Are class distinctions (*a*) inevitable, (*b*) desirable ?
Medieval idea of each man occupying a definite place
in the social scale. He knew what it was and was content
with it. Although there have been many moves from one
class to another, we have distinct social classes, not based,
as in America, so much on income as on method of
living, and outlook. Money can provide the necessary
surroundings, but not the outlook. There is also a
division according to income. Thus better education,
accommodation, etc., reserved for those who can pay for it
Very often the upper social class also is in the upper
income class. Effect of the War on class distinction
Change in income level. One finds people in expensive
restaurants and clubs who before the War would not
have been there. After the War, when their incomes
shrink, will they resume their old social habits ? Will
the new contacts made, especially in the ranks, owing to
conscription, cause a social levelling process ? What will
be the effect of the new educational opportunities that
may be afforded ? Will there always be the class apart,
consisting of current celebrities ? Intellectual distinction
there must be, owing to uneven mental development.
There will always be at least one class apart. Will there,
and should there be others ?

14. *What Form should Youth Organizations take after the War?*

Youth organizations at present in existence. Scouts. Military Organizations. Clubs started by Cinemas. Purpose—to train in citizenship, to occupy leisure time usefully, to train for war, to inculcate idea of service to the State. Are all these approved by the group? If not, why? The nature of the aim considered desirable will determine the nature of the organization. Should membership be compulsory, as in the Hitler Youth? Should emphasis be on discipline of individual, or character training, or provision of practical and useful knowledge? If conscription remains.after the War, what will be the relation between Militia and these Youth Groups?

15. *Uncontrolled Advertising is a Social Evil*

Function of advertising? To sell at all costs, irrespective of demand, or to state excellency of a product so that public may know that a particular need can be met? Present method. Forced demand more often than not. War-time advertising—to keep public attention fixed on the products a firm used to produce, and hopes to produce after the War. Dishonest tricks in advertising. Exploitation of our emotions and instincts—i.e., fear, pride, snobbery, greed. Mesmeric advertisements, depending for success on repetition of single command or statement. (Leader should ask members to bring advertisements for the group to analyse.) Ask such questions as: How does advertisement achieve its purpose? Method used? How much does it tell you about a product? What proof is offered? What proof should be offered?

SECTION II—Educational

1. *Boarding or Day Schools?*

Two main factors are to be considered here: (1) Is the parent capable of bringing up the child, and the proper person to do so ? (2) Is a child at a disadvantage if brought up by himself with few opportunities of mixing with those of his own age ? In a large family, or where a child can have many friends, a boarding school would seem less necessary. But since teachers are specialists, can parents do the job of bringing up a child as well ? Effect of return home from a nursery school to be considered. Strong case for boarding school where home atmosphere not suitable for satisfactory development of child. Try to get opinions of those who have been to boarding and day schools.

2. *Is an International Language Necessary ?*

Here an introduction is necessary. Outline attempts at forming an International Language, and give salient features of Esperanto, Basic English, and Hogben's " Interglossa " (see Penguin Books). Define purpose of such a language. (1) Get group to decide whether such a language is desirable—for commercial and normal social requirements, i.e., by tourists, merchants, and others. Will such a language make for better relationships between nations ? Why has no such language been universally adopted before ? If group agree that all nations should be at least bi-lingual—their own, and the new language for travelling purposes, decide (2) of what type it is to be. Esperanto is an artificial language and dead. " Interglossa " is living, and much of it is familiar. Both are not natural   " Basic " is, and criticisms such as why foist English on us—why can't it be French, German, etc., must be met. (3) Then decide how the chosen language is to be made universal.

Note re " Basic." An Englishman must know the limits of its vocabulary, otherwise he will not be understood.

3. *Is State Control of Education Desirable ?*

French system, whereby curriculum determined by Minister of Education : Ensures that a minimum is studied—state-controlled exams. returns, etc. English methods : Elementary and Secondary schools ; dual control by Ministry of Education Inspectorate—reports and recommendations ; local municipal control by Board of Managers—often incapable by reason of lack of knowledge, to control or debate educational matters. Other schools recognized by M. of E.—subject to inspections. New Bill brings all schools under Ministry as far as Inspectors are concerned. Considerable latitude allowed to headmasters of Elementary and Secondary schools. Standard maintained by control ? Private schools, which are not recognized by M. of E., often leave much to be desired. Can an outsider, not conversant with difficulties and problems of a headmaster, judge adequately as a result of a two days' inspection ? Damaging nature of adverse reports, based on watching a few lessons. Incompetence of Boards of Governors, composed of municipal councillors. The State could do far more by acting in an advisory capacity—providing experts on various subjects to give help, to sponsor and suggest schemes, and to provide material, etc.

At present, educational publication is in the hands of the commercial firms, and such books are produced for profit. State should encourage educational research. B.B.C. does a good work for education—semi-State-controlled organization. No co-ordination of work of B.B.C., Universities, and commercial firms.

4. *Is there any Justification for the Teaching of Dead Languages ?*

It all depends on what the individual wants to be after he has left school. If he has to, or wants to take an Arts or a Medical Course at a University, Latin is necessary, as a credit in this subject must be secured at Matriculation. Latin terminology widely used by medical profession. Is it necessary to spend many years learning Latin solely to be able to understand certain technical terms ? Can literature and language be appreciated if one has

49

no classical background? Language study is made much easier owing to the many Latin derivations. Translation from and into Latin is a valuable training in method and expression. An acquaintance through language with the classical ideal is valuable as a guide to conduct. For a man's experience to be as full as possible—if he is going to study an Arts subject especially—acquaintance with the classics is very desirable. For those of a scientific and mechanical turn of mind, or who show no aptitude, the study should be stopped at once, and attention turned to something more profitable. The study of the classics should never be allowed to become a drudgery; what is learned then is soon forgotten, and a subject more valuable to the individual will provide a similar mental discipline.

5. *Poetry is a Waste of Time*

Certainly, if badly taught, as is too often the case. This is the cause of much dislike of poetry. Value of poetry: (1) Reveals new experiences and known objects in a new light. Experience is richer as a result of this sharing. (2) Joy in descriptive phrase and vivid or unusual choice of words. (3) Delight in sound and pictures presented by the poet. (4) "Art is a choice." We are able to learn what is significant for the poet and achieve thereby a scale of values with which to compare our own. (5) We all have an instinctive delight in rhythm.

Consider why the view stated above, that poetry is a waste of time, is held. Then discuss how points (1)-(5) above may be illustrated, so that children may leave school with a liking for poetry. Deal with the importance of getting children to write poetry as a means of teaching them to appreciate efforts of others, and as a training in self-expression.

6. *Should English Spelling be Reformed?*

To whom does English spelling give difficulty? To what extent do we feel that the immense work of reform that would be required is really necessary? Would our work be so very much easier if reform were undertaken ? Is a vast amount of time spent learning how to spell in school ?

Our spelling is the result of development ; every form has its history and its reason. To change spelling is to obscure the derivation of a word, which in some cases is a useful " anchor," keeping it from being used too far from its original meaning. Lack of clear connection (e.g., Latin *nescius*, and present day derivative " nice "). means gradual deterioration of the word. What does " nice " mean to-day ? There are many exceptions, but this is one method of bringing home the real meaning of a word. If spelling were changed a word might get mixed up with another of similar spelling, and might lose its meaning, e.g., " embalm "—re-spell embarm—mixed up with medieval " barm " (bosom), becomes " to embosom " What do we do for a word to express original " embalm " ? Possibilities, phonetic spelling. If Basic English is adopted, is need for spelling reform more justified then ? For Basic English only ? Difficulties of two spellings.

7. *Co-Education is the only Worthwhile Form of Education*

Education to prepare for life ; segregation of the sexes causes child to be brought up in artificial surroundings. Adjustment is necessary later, when he leaves school, sometimes with unfortunate results.

Being brought up with girls brings a boy into contact with those female qualities which are desirable—gentleness, tenderness, etc. A girl can acquire masculine qualities of independence, adventure, etc. Moral difficulties encountered at a later stage.

Mental development of the two sexes. Danger of rivalry and jealousy.

8. *Public Schools are a Hindrance to Educational Reform*

What has the Public School to offer that a Secondary School has not ? Religious background ; a " Christian " education instead of a purely secular one. A corporate life lived among beautiful buildings. A sense of tradition and loyalty to the group. A staff with often a wider background than is the case in non-Public Schools.

Undue stress on games—a fetish made of them at times ? Too exclusive, owing to high fees. Government based on the " leader principle." Too fascist for adequate preparation for life in a democratic community ? Often little interest shown in the unintelligent boy—the brilliant only catered for.

House system, where the house owned by the House Master, and run by him for private profit, sometimes at the expense of the pupils.

Class distinction and snobbery fostered unconsciously ? How to make available for all the advantages of a public school education ? Should there be a class education— should there be schools for all, to which children must go irrespective of income of parents ?

9. *Education Should be less Liberal and More Technical*

A man must be able to earn his living. ˙Should schools teach a trade or profession, or prepare in any way for one ? What is the value of mere factual knowledge, which is easily forgotten ? Is it enough to teach how to reason, and to inculcate the three R's ? Are these the minimum requirements ? If so, what else should be added ? Cultural subjects to increase enjoyment, and ensure a fuller life, or technical subjects to train the hands and prepare for future employment ? Some children never benefit by academic courses. They must learn by doing, being practically minded. Should they be trained according to their aptitude and individual pre- ferences ? If no particular aptitude is shown, who will decide the nature of a child's education ? Will both sides be catered for equally, the technical and cultural ? Wrong emphasis to be avoided. The narrow outlook of the specialist undesirable.

10. *Parents are Unfitted to bring up Their own Children*

Bringing up children is a specialized job, requiring considerable study; added to knowledge there is also a need for adequate provision of accommodation, so that the child may develop in surroundings that are suitable. Only recently has there been any organized instruction in parenthood. How many parents make a real study of the treatment of children—of their bodies and minds? Do they know the correct way to deal with such problems as lying, stealing, desire to know about the body, religious matters, etc.? How many can provide nurseries? If children of the poor go to nursery schools, and are taught correct behaviour there, much of the work is undone when the child returns home for the holidays. Many families are too large, and the parent hasn't the time and patience to deal with each child as she should. Refer to public treatment of children in crowded places. How often are children seen (improperly clad) eating bread and jam in the streets? Should parents be prohibited from bringing up children unless they can prove that they are capable of doing so?

11. *What is the Purpose of Education?*

Many definitions—much misconception. Get answers from those concerned with education if possible. Then discuss them.

Is education a process that goes on all one's life, or is it confined to the period spent at school? Who educates? Books, teacher, one's acquaintances? Is it synonymous with book learning—factual knowledge? Can one be learned and yet un-educated? Is it synonymous with teaching? Education is experience; a continual process. The educated man is the experienced man. His reactions are quicker, more satisfactory. Is education concerned with morals? Is a man who has much evil experience educated? Is there good and bad education (in the moral sense)? Consider the term, " A religious education." If education is experience, what experiences are considered desirable during school years ? How can they best be obtained ? Acquaintance through books with well-educated men and women of the past—poets and prose writers ? Experience gained as a result of ." doing." Placing a child in many different situations, and noting reactions. Approximating those experiences to those which a child will meet in later life.

12. *Religious Instruction Should be an Essential Element of Education*

Two types of school to consider, the secular and the denominational school. Are the ends sought by all denominations the making more perfect and harmonious both the individual and therefore the community ? Do they teach the Sermon on the Mount, and the Golden Rule as a code of conduct ? If this is kept for Sundays, and not made the centre round which one's life should revolve, and to which all actions should be related, it loses much of its value. Is it, therefore, introduced into the schools as an ideal code of conduct to be kept continually before everyone's eyes ? In a denominational school, is anything else presented, contrary to this ? Are those who teach religion qualified, and do they practise what they teach ? In the secular school, can any form of religious teaching be presented, without denominational bias ? The simplest references to Jesus must bear some evidence of the individual's attitude to Him, an attitude determined by his religious beliefs, or lack of them. Is the " agreed syllabus " framed to teach religion—if so, what " brand " of religion ? Is there such a thing as undenominational religious teaching ? Does not such become ethical instruction only ?

13. *Should Children be Allowed to Choose their own Subjects ?*

A child learns more quickly, and better, if the incentive comes from within, and is not imposed from without. His desire to know will act as an incentive, and so he will discipline himself in order to acquire the desired knowledge. Does a child, at an early age, really know what he wants to study? What happens to the child who doesn't want to study anything? Will a child choose the easiest subjects? Will he tire quickly, and take up subject after subject? A great deal of time is wasted by his being made to learn what he doesn't like, and what he will soon forget. Artificial method of cutting periods into 45-minute divisions, and having to study at a set time a new subject, when he is perhaps interested in the last lesson, and would like to carry on by himself.

14. *Children Should not be Allowed to go to the Cinema until they leave School*

On the screen, we often see a world of false values; crime is glorified; sentimentality abounds; undue prominence is given to infidelity. Most films are designed for adults, many of whom have no artistic sense or real taste, but who want to be amused, and who desire to react spontaneously to what they see. They do not want to be made to think. Their lives are dull, and they want to enjoy romance vicariously. Is this the type of "entertainment" we want children to see? The pictures leave a vivid impression on the child mind, and tend to destroy anything of value derived from education of the mind and spirit through literature, art and music.

Should children be "nursed" until they leave school? Will there not be a great shock when they see the world as it is? Will not the realization, gained by seeing films, that crime and infidelity exist, cause them to turn against it, and to adhere more closely to established codes of behaviour? If so, will these things be an entertainment any longer? Should the child not be allowed to decide its own cultural level? Will not that be the test of the success of its education? The success of the commercial film is partly due to the fact that the mass of the public have never had an opportunity of seeing films that could be termed "classics."

15. *Examinations Should be Abolished*

Examinations are often an unfair test. Many children never acquire the examination technique. Their memories are poor, or they suffer from nervousness. The choice of question is often limited, and a child is not given an opportunity to show what he knows. Marking is a subjective process depending on the state of the individual mind at the moment. Is anything done to remedy this? Two people marking same paper? An essay which seems good to one individual is considered poor by another.

Many qualities desirable in an individual cannot be examined. An examination gives no evidence of reliability, initiative, etc. An employer requires some knowledge of this, yet individuals are engaged because they have a good examination record.

Should examinations be regarded as informal affairs to provide the student with a method of testing his own knowledge? Would Universities be satisfied with a certificate from a Headmaster showing aptitude of a pupil, and some indication as to standard reached during period at school? Would this do instead of University examinations?

SECTION III—Political

1. *Are we a Democracy?*

Start by questions. Who governs us? List answers on blackboard on one side, and draw a diagram of a triangle and insert, at appropriate levels from base upwards, various governing bodies. Public as voters, House of Commons, House of Lords, Cabinet, King. Add Local Government, etc. Draw diagram in reply to such questions as how does an M.P. get elected? People vote—those over twenty-one. State those who cannot vote. How many do they elect? Is the House of Commons the only governing body? No, House of Lords. How are they chosen? Continue with others.

Who has ultimate power ? Treasury ? Monied interests ?
People ? Who could we do without ? House of Lords ?
What is its function ? Should it be abolished ? (this
could make a separate discussion). Is it true to say that
no one person has the real control, that all work together
as a whole ?

2. Is Dictatorship an Evil ?

Distinguish between theory and practice. If you had
a dictator who was loved, and who acted on behalf of the
majority wisely and with moderation, would that not be
better than a timorous, ineffective democratic government ? What are theoretical merits of dictatorship ?
Speed of action ; unity of policy. Are there any others ?
What do the Fascists say about this type of Government ?
Demerits : Fallibility of individual ; necessity to keep
confidence of multitude—by force or showmanship ;
people often dragooned not led.

Is there a middle way ? Dictatorship by a Group.
Charles II and his Cabal. Roman Triumvirate. The
solution : A recognition that the Government is the
executive of the people, whether it be one, three, or many.
The people must be articulate. They must register their
opinion, and make sure that their Government is in their
interests. How is this to be done ? (Subject for another
discussion—" How can the majority make its wishes
known ? ")

3. Can we Justify our Empire ?

Is the possession of an Empire consonant with
being a democracy ? Foreign misunderstandings. The
constituent members of the Empire : Dominions—self-
governing ; India—direct and indirect control exercised
by Viceroy and cabinet ; Colonies—some self-governing,
some directly controlled by Britain. Smaller number
than those not controlled. Eire neutral in War. Comment
on this. What right had we ever to acquire territory

to which we may have given, or been forced to yield, self-government ? Could the backward colonial peoples govern themselves ? Are we preparing them for the time when they can ? What would happen if we left India ? What advantages has British rule brought ?

4. Are the Dominions Really Free ?

What is the rôle of the Crown ? King acts on advice of Dominion Ministers, who are answerable to the people of that Dominion. Dominion Parliament makes its laws, which are binding on its own people. Provisions of Statute of Westminster should be referred to. All except Eire decided to join Great Britain in the war against Germany. Should there be any retaliatory measures against Eire ? Dominion leaders consult. Is there any evidence that British policy or Cabinet exercises undue influence on Dominion policy ? At Geneva, Dominions sometimes voted differently. Are there some occasions, as at League meetings, where a united front is desirable ?

Are there economic ties which bind Dominions to this country ? Control of policy by interested groups of large shareholders ?

The question of a close federation might profitably be discussed. Concerted action and policy, instead of individual action.

5. The House of Lords should be Abolished

No control over entry. Depends on birth, or creation of peerages. Its members are not representative of the majority. House can seriously delay passage of a Bill. Expense—i.e., provision of accommodation, etc. Lords do not receive salaries. Episcopal peers. Are they qualified to discuss politics ?

Lords exercise curb on dangerous legislation (dangerous to whom ?) Owing to fact that many have much leisure, they can become experts in a subject, and their opinion is valuable. They tend to discuss more calmly, in an academic and impersonal atmosphere. Do they see problems from angles different from those from which members of the Commons see them ? Do they study questions more impersonally ?

6. *How to Reform the Electoral System*

Representation now based on geographical areas. Population moves, so when more people enter an area the number of representatives remains the same. All groups and interests in the one area have one representative—should an M.P. represent a section of the community only ? So many for lawyers, schoolmasters, tradesmen, etc. Chamber of Corporations. Advantages of this method. Allot one member to so many individuals. An M.P. often knows his locality well, and the type of persons in it ; is in the best position to look after the interests of such a group. Proportional representation and its advantages. The University and Business vote— one man has two M.P.s to represent him. Is this fair ? Advantages of money at elections. Difficulties in setting up as a candidate. The Party machine and the prospective candidate.

7. *Post-War Treatment of Germany*

Did we act unwisely after the last war ? Dismemberment into states, repression, armies of occupation ? Are German tendencies inherent ? Can they be eradicated, or continually repressed ? Can Prussianism, and desire to be the master race, be changed by an educational process ? Can anything be done with Nazi Youth, or should one concentrate on next generation ? Who will dictate type of government the Germans should have ? Are they ever to be allowed to take their place in European Councils as an equal ?

8. *How should War Criminals be Treated ?*

Define war criminals. Purpose in dealing with criminals. Is it mere revenge ? Is any useful purpose served by administering what is called "justice"? Will punishment deter others? War criminals would be dangerous if left at large. What charge is to be brought against them? What is the authority required to decide their fault? An International Court? Treatment of an official who was merely obeying orders, however cruel. Is he to blame, or the person who framed the orders? Did he not in his turn consider that he was doing his duty? Generals wage total war. Such warfare admits of no humane sentiment. Are our Bomber Command to be tried because they have bombed civilians? Or not to be tried, solely because we have won the war? Is it possible to isolate and punish instances of deliberate and unnecessary brutality indulged in for its own sake? Position of the leaders—Hitler, Mussolini? Is it a legal crime to start a war? Not according to International Law. Should we frame an international code of law, and provide an International Court, sanctioned by all nations, so that heads of states could be brought to trial? Could the provision of such a code be made retrospective?

9. Why does War Start?

Rival nationalities? Too many sovereign states? Mere lust for power? Adoption of Balance of Power as a counter measure to domination in one country? Inability to sell a country's products, therefore necessity to manufacture armaments, which have a ready sale, and must be used to ensure a constant stream of production? Conflicting doctrines? War ideological?

U.S.A. and Canada have never fought, though living side by side. Do they see the futility of war, while other countries do not?

Is there a genuine belief held in some countries that war is glorious, and a legitimate device to attain one's own ends? Are some races so mentally constituted that they are incapable of living in peace?

Analyse the known causes of such wars as the Thirty Years' Religious wars ; invasion of England by William I ; Richard II's expeditions against Ireland ; Crusades.

10. *How can War be Stopped ?*

Can it be made physically impossible for a nation to fight ? Total abolition of armaments, under international supervision ? Would nations still find other methods of fighting ? Sanctions and reprisals—police methods by an International Police Force ? Would people want to fight if they had all their needs supplied and could see that it was not in their interests to destroy what they had gained ? Could the mental causes be made ineffective by education ? Could the coming generation be educated to regard war as not worth while ? Great powers should be made to feel that it is their responsibility to see that smaller states are protected from aggression and are able to lead the sort of lives they wish to.

11. *What should be the Future of our Colonial Empires ?*

Start by stating what our colonies are, and how governed. What we have done, and what we get out of them. Give facts—statistics.

Should we hand over Colonies to an International Commission ? This Commission would re-allocate them as mandates, and lay down definite instructions as to how they should be treated. Provision of inspection—League of Nations to control ? Who will control the Commission—who will decide ? What will be the position of investors who have interests in our Colonies ? Is there any reason why we should change our present method of administration ? Have we any right to be in control of colonies at all ? Should we adopt a more positive conception of trusteeship, and not rest content until all were living as we should like to live ? Should such development be left to the colonials themselves ? Are colonies a disadvantage to us ? Who pays for increasing standard of living there ? Separate developments for different races living in the same colony ? Should we relinquish all control, and only assume it again if invited by colonials themselves to do so ?

12. *Is a Federated Europe Possible ?*

Compare U.S.A. and U.S.S.R., and the proposed Federation of European States. In the first there is some similarity of racial origin—one ideal binds all the States ; in U.S.S.R., an ideal binds all ; is there any link that might bind European States ? Determination to maintain a future peace ? Would all States be willing to limit their sovereignty to a central authority ? Necessity for adoption of a settled economic and foreign policy. Could such countries as those in Europe, with such divergent pasts and outlooks, ever agree to pool resources and adopt one currency, etc. ? Language difficulty. If no Federation, what is the alternative ? A Federation of the Scandinavian democracies and ourselves ? Maintenance of old system of balance of power.

13. *Should we make People more Politically-Minded ?*

If we are to be a democracy, we should exercise our power to have a say in the determination of events. Has one time to undertake the necessary study ? Would our protest be of any avail ? Are people going to take an interest in politics unless they are assured of the value of their actions. Popular apathy. Leave it to professional politicians—" I can't be bothered " attitude. Should people be forced to vote ? Should popular instruction be given in schools and during working hours (e.g., War-time factory discussions) ? Many consider politics a " dirty game." Should we get rid of this attitude (at least) ? Only a few newspapers report politics seriously. Should the Press be asked to help in the spread of political education ? How often are M.P.s required to report to their constituents as a whole ? How often do constituents write to their M.P., and follow his parliamentary activities on their behalf ?

14. *To what Extent are we a Group of United Nations?*

٭ American Lease and Lend Act. Altruism, or enlightened nationalism? Pooling of national resources. Reciprocal aid. Hospitality to foreign troops. Books circulated explaining differences between nations, and advice as to how to understand one another. Overseas Reception Board Scheme for evacuation of children. Clothing and necessities sent from U.S.A. and by us to Russia. German methods to dis-unite Allies. Are they listened to? What are they? List, and examine them. (1) Separate peace will be concluded between any two; (2) Allies will institute communism; (3) U.S.A. want to secure financial domination; (4) Britain desires only to maintain the *status quo*, etc. Are we as united with U.S.S.R. as with U.S.A.? What can be done now, and after the War, to cement union even further?

15. *How can Opinion be Influenced?*

First, there must be knowledge. Individuals should study and discuss—this is where discussion groups come in. Mere discussion, however, is not enough.

When agreement is reached on some social or political question, what can be done to implement that decision? Would anyone take notice of protests, letters to papers, petitions and deputations to M.P.s? If on a large enough scale, is opinion influenced? Demands for increased Service pay. Result? Protest against Hoare-Laval Peace Pact. Result? Formation of societies, whose members are well-informed as a result of discussion and study. Such societies are in a better position, by reason of their status and numbers, to influence opinion. Necessity for keeping a watch on activities of M.P.s. Activity in connection with political organizations. Local Party Committee; Party Conferences. Much can be done through Party Organization. Local action similar and easier. Pressure brought to bear on Town Councils.

APPENDIX I

SOME FURTHER SUBJECTS FOR DISCUSSION

1. Is Poverty Inevitable ?
2. Can Unemployment be Prevented ?
3. Should Children do Homework ?
4. What is Free Thinking ?
5. Does Christianity demand a New Society, or Society demand a new Christianity ?
6. Do we need a National Theatre ?
7. A Statesman who Cannot Change His Mind can have no Mind to Change.
8. Does it Matter what Kind of English we Write
9. Should University Graduates be Accounted Superior Persons and Accorded a Special Position in Society ?
10. The more Millionaires, the Better for Everyone.
11. Civilization has Destroyed the Spirit of Adventure.
12. The Hire-Purchase System is more often a Curse than a Blessing.
13. A Man who Reads Romantic Love Stories at the age of Forty has Failed to Grow Up.
14. Should Parents give their Children Complete Freedom ?
15. The Inventor is the Enemy of the People, because He Causes Unemployment.
16. Free Trade is Preferable to Tariff-Protected Trade.
17. Should Capital Punishment be Abolished ?
18. A Party Government is Preferable to a National one.
19. Should Land Ownership be Controlled ?
20. India should be Given Self-Government.
21. The worst Enemies of the English Language are the English People.
22. All Employees should Share in a Firm's Profits.
23. The School-Leaving Age should be Raised to Seventeen.

24. Should we Allow Banking to Remain in Private Hands ?
25. England should be, as far as possible, a Self-Supporting Unit.

APPENDIX II

BOOKS FOR REFERENCE AND FURTHER READING

Some Useful Series :

1.	Oxford Pamphlets on World Affairs	Various authors	O.U.P.
2.	Oxford Pamphlets on Home Affairs •	,,	O.U.P.
3.	Macmillan War Pamphlets	,,	Macmillan
4.	Pamphlets on the Commonwealth	,,	Longmans
5.	Penguin Specials ...	,,	Penguin
6.	Democratic Order Series	,,	Kegan Paul
7.	British Life and Thought	,,	Longmans
8.	Nelson Discussion Books	,,	Nelson
9.	Current Problems ...	,,	C.U.P.
10.	" World To-day " Series	,,	O.U.P.
11.	Britain in Pictures ...	..	Collins
12.	Handbooks for Discussion Groups	,,	Assn. for Education in Citizenship
13.	W.E.A. Study Outlines		W.E.A.
14.	Fabian Research Series...	,,	Fabian Publications

On Reasoning and Argument :

1.	Straight and Crooked Thinking	Thouless	E.U.P.
2.	Straight and Crooked Thinking in War-Time	Thouless	E.U.P.
3.	Tyranny of Words ...	Chase	Methuen
4.	Thinking to Some Purpose	Stebbing	Pelican
5.	Reading and Reasoning...	Musson	Crowther

6.	Propaganda	Lambert	Nelson
✓ 7.	How to Think Clearly ...	Jepson	Longmans

Social :

1.	Christianity and Social Order	Temple	Penguin
2.	Christian Behaviour ...	Lewis	Bles
3.	Broadcast Talks ...	Lewis	Bles
4.	Screwtape Letters ...	Lewis	Bles
5.	Brave New World ...	Haxley	Chatto
6.	The Two Moralities ...	Lindsay	Eyre and Spottiswoode
7.	Our Own Times ...	King Hall	Nicholson & Watson
8.	English Saga	Bryant	Collins
9.	St George and the Dragon	Elton	Collins
10.	Health of the Future ...	Bourne	Penguin
11.	Britain's Health ...	P.E.P.	Pelican
12.	Parents' Revolt ...	R. and K. Titmuss	Secker and Warburg
13.	The British Social Services	Owen	Longmans
14.	Report on Social Insurance and Allied Services	Beveridge	H.M.S.O.
15.	The Fifth Arm	Wickham Steed	Constable
16.	The Press	Cummings	Lane
17.	Broadcasting	Matheson	Butterworth
18.	Radio is Changing Us ...	Thompson	Watts
19.	Town and Country To-morrow	Bounphrey	Nelson
20.	In Quest of Justice ...	Mullins	Murray
21.	Report of the Committee on Land Utilization in Rural Areas. (The " Scott " Report)	—	H.M.S.O.

22.	Report of the Expert Committee on Compensation and Betterment. (The "Uthwatt" Report)	—	H.M.S.O.
23.	Report of the Royal Commission on the Distribution of Industrial Population. (The "Barlow" Report)	—	H.M.S.O.

Education :

1.	Outline of the Structure of the Educational System in England and Wales	—	H.M.S.O.
2.	Bias and Education for Democracy	Stewart	O.U.P.
3.	The Future of Education	Livingstone	C.U.P.
4.	Education for Citizenship	Barker	O.U.P.
5.	A New Order in English Education	Dent	U.L.P.
6.	The Education of a Community	Stead	U.L.P.
7.	Education for Democracy	Cohen and Travers	Routledge
8.	Education for Democracy	Margaret Cole	Fabian Society
9.	Education for the People	Spencer	Routledge

Political and Economic :

1.	Twenty Years' Crisis ...	Carr	Macmillan
2.	The Conditions of Peace	Carr	Macmillan
3.	Peace by Power ...	Gelber	O.U.P.
4.	Private Enterprise or Public Control	Robinson	E.U.P.

5.	Industry after the War...	Madge	Pilot Press
6.	International Economics	Harrod	C.U.P.
7.	Reconstruction	F.B.I.	Macmillan
8.	Practical Economics ...	Cole	Pelican
✓ 9.	The Theory of Money ...	Barker	C.U.P.
10.	British Agriculture ...	Astor and Rowntree	Penguin
✓ 11.	The Argument of Empire	Hancock	Penguin
12.	Germany Puts the Clock Back	Mowrer	Penguin
13.	Inside Europe	Gunther	Hamilton
14.	Nazi Germany Explained	Vernon Bartlett	Gollancz
15.	The Future of Nations...	Carr	Routledge
16.	I Believe in Democracy	Lindsay	O.U.P.
17.	The Government of Britain	Young	Collins
18.	The Post-War House of Commons	Turner	Craig and Wilson
19.	The Councillor ...	Shelley	Nelson

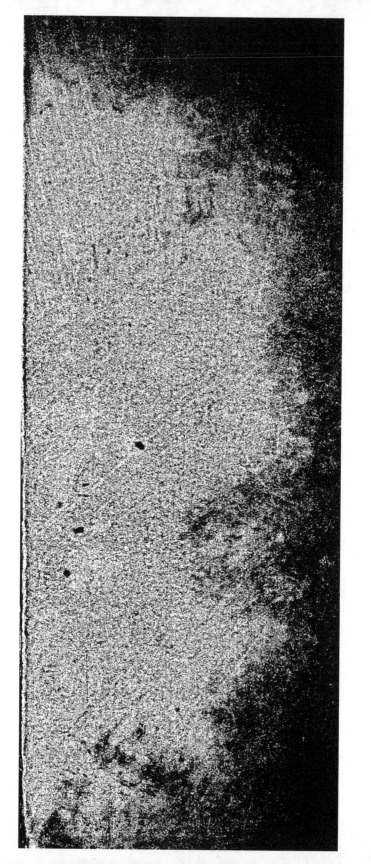

CPSIA information can be obtained
at www.ICGtesting.com
Printed in the USA
BVHW08*1525041018
529297BV00008B/174/P